Original title:
Pine Needles and Puns

Copyright © 2025 Creative Arts Management OÜ
All rights reserved.

Author: Ronan Whitfield
ISBN HARDBACK: 978-1-80567-236-4
ISBN PAPERBACK: 978-1-80567-535-8

## **Frond Funfair**

At the fair, the fronds do twirl,
With laughter loud, they spin and whirl.
A leaf beside a beetle pranced,
In this green world, all are entranced.

A silly squirrel in a tree,
Tries to dance, oh wobbly spree!
His acorns fly, much to his dread,
While giggles bounce from branch to head.

With every twist, a chuckle bursts,
As nature's humor freely thrusts.
A flower tells a joke so sly,
Even passing clouds stop by.

So come one, come all, to this delight,
Where every glance brings sheer delight.
In frond-filled funfair, there's no rush,
Just let the laughter flow in a hush.

## **Needlepoint Nonsense**

In the forest, threads intertwine,
Stitching stories, oh so fine.
A hedgehog knits with prickly glee,
While bumblebees hum harmoniously.

A wobbly deer with fashion flair,
Wears a scarf made from old air.
Said a crow, "Oh what a sight!
You really need to fly, not fight!"

With pine-cones bouncing in bright hues,
They play tag among the morning dews.
A wise old owl chimed in to say,
"Needlepoint nonsense brightens the day!"

So gather round for laughter's blend,
In this realm where quirks transcend.
With every stitch, the stories spin,
In needlepoint nonsense, we all win!

## **Aromatic Antics**

In a forest filled with zest,
A tree took on a quest.
It wore a crown of green,
Claiming it was quite the scene.

With every gust, a whiff so bold,
Tickled noses young and old.
Whispered jokes upon the breeze,
Sending giggles through the trees.

## Sapling Satire

A sprout once said to an oak so grand,
"You're like a beard, you really should stand!"
The oak just chuckled, swayed with glee,
"At least I'm not short; that's plain to see!"

The little one replied, a grin so wide,
"Just means I'm closer to the wild ride!"
A banter echoed all around,
In the heart of the woods, humor's found.

## The Branching Joke

Two branches met at a sunny top,
One said, "Let's go, make the leaves hop!"
The other quipped, with a leafy grin,
"Only if you can wiggle out the skin!"

The trees laughed loud, their limbs intertwined,
Telling tales of the birds and the time they dined.
With each soft whisper, a hearty jest,
In this forest, humor's truly blessed.

## Needled Wit

A quirky shrub with a witty twist,
Proposed to star in a comedy list.
"Would you like to hear a joke or two?"
"Only if I don't get pruned, it's true!"

In the shade, the laughter grew,
As prickly puns continually flew.
Needles sharp, but spirits high,
In the garden of jest, they'll always fly.

## Humor Under the Boughs

In the forest, laughter rings,
A squirrel dressed in random things,
Chasing shadows, making haste,
His punchlines gone without a trace.

The branches sway, a comical act,
As the wind tells jokes, a harmless pact,
Birds chirp in witty retort,
Nature's stand-up, a funny sport.

Frogs croak puns by the brook,
While deer stop to take a look,
A rabbit takes the mic, so sly,
Cracking jokes with a twinkle in his eye.

Underneath the leafy crowns,
Humor grows, abolishing frowns,
Laughter echoes, free and vast,
A comedy show, with nature cast.

## Quips from the Conifers

Amongst the evergreens so tall,
You might just hear a quippy call,
A wise owl hoots a playful tease,
While chipmunks giggle in the breeze.

The breeze whispers cheeky tales,
Of critters who've mastered silly trails,
A hedgehog snickers, sharp and spry,
Witty remarks made on the fly.

Cedar trees lean in to hear,
The antics of the woodland, clear,
Their needles rustle, in delight,
With each good pun, the stars ignite.

As sunbeams dance through airy space,
Beneath the boughs, the jokes embrace,
In this realm, where spirits swirl,
The laughter of the forest unfurl.

## **An Evergreen Laugh**

In a wooded realm of vibrant green,
Witty whispers, a lively scene,
With nature's charm, the humor flows,
As trees exchange their clever prose.

A bumblebee with a daring grin,
Buzzes jokes, and shares a spin,
The ants march on with glee and pride,
Their tiny jokes they do not hide.

Foxes play pranks in moonlit glades,
While raccoons charm with quick charades,
The forest floor is where you'll find,
A reservoir of laughs combined.

Every branch chuckles under the sun,
Where laughter lives, and joy's not done,
In this arena of jolly cheer,
Mirth echoes loud for all to hear.

## The Cheery Canopy

Beneath the canopy so bright,
Jokes are shared from morn till night,
The squirrels leap, a pun-filled race,
Chasing laughter all over the place.

A curious owl, with a wink of eye,
Delivers jests as the clouds float by,
With every swish of a leafy tail,
Nature's humor lifts the veil.

The sun peeks through with a sunny grin,
Lighting the way for good times to begin,
Woodpeckers tap a rhythm so jaunty,
Creating fits of laughter so plenty.

In this grove of jovial sights,
Where joy dances on tree-top heights,
With every rustle, without a care,
Life's a joke, let's all share!

## The Hilarious Hush of the Forest

In the woods, the trees they sway,
Chirping jokes, come out and play.
Squirrels giggle, oh what a sight,
As branches dance in pure delight.

Frogs croak puns, they croon with glee,
Bees buzz laughter, wild and free.
The breeze tickles the leaves so bright,
Even the shadows join the light.

## Witty Whispers in the Woods

Mice tell tales of cheese and cream,
While owls plot the ultimate scheme.
Trees wear grins, their bark a tease,
Nature's humor flows with ease.

A hedgehog snorts at a twig's bad pun,
While sunbeams break, just having fun.
Twisting paths hide cheeky views,
As whimsy paints the morning hues.

## **Treetop Tittering: A Tall Tale**

Beetles boast of flying high,
Claiming wings were meant to fly.
A raccoon wearing a tiny hat,
Makes everyone giggle at that!

High above, the secrets spill,
As crow and sparrow chase a thrill.
Underneath the laughing boughs,
They join the chant of nature's vows.

## Laughter Laced with Aromatic Pines

The scent of jest lingers sweet,
Sassy ferns sway on their feet.
Spruce trees chuckle, evergreen jest,
Their needles glitter, nature's best.

In every rustle, a playful cheer,
As laughter echoes, it draws us near.
A wind-up squirrel, a punchline so grand,
In my leafy realm, laughter's always planned.

## Quirky Quercus

In a forest where laughter grows,
A tree with jokes that only it knows.
Its branches wiggled with flair,
Tickling squirrels in mid-air.

Leaves gossip when breezes come by,
Whispering secrets, oh my, oh my!
A nut fell down, but it grinned,
"I'm cracking up!" it chimed as it twinned.

Mushrooms below chuckle in glee,
Spreading humor as light as can be.
The roots tap dance with glee so bright,
Every shadow a giggle in the night.

## Twisted Branches

A crooked trunk in a forest bold,
Holds tales of laughter, stories untold.
Raccoons play tricks on this fine tree,
Leaving behind a riddle, you see?

Its branches wave with a quirky twist,
"Join the fun!" they insist,
Each knot and turn, a punchline made,
In this wood, worries just fade.

Acorns fall like jokes from above,
Making the whole woodland giggle in love.
Saplings snicker at the old bark's charm,
While squirrels laugh, all cozy and warm.

## Silvan Silliness

In a glen that gleams with joy so rare,
Trees conspire in the cool, crisp air.
Sticks play hopscotch in a lively row,
As fellow flora puts on a show.

The foliage chuckles, don't you see?
Each leaf a jest, most humorously.
A thistle chimed in, "I'm sharp as a tack!"
While daisies danced, their petals a snack.

Even the shadows join in the jest,
As sunbeams tickle, they stand out best.
This woodland stage holds a grand display,
Where every joke keeps gloom at bay.

## **Woody Whims**

In the woodland of whimsical delight,
Bark wears a grin, so cheerful and bright.
Each stump shows off its rugged old style,
While nuts roll by with a mischievous smile.

Twisted twigs tell tales of cheer,
Echoing laughter for all to hear.
The forest floor is a giggle trap,
While critters gather for a nap (or a rap).

Roots play tag in a dance with flair,
Branches join in, swinging through air.
With each rustling leaf, a new jest is spun,
A woodsy party where everyone's fun!

## Whispers from the Evergreen Carpet

Amid the branches green, they tease,
A carpet soft that whispers with ease.
Fallen bits with stories to share,
In the forest's laughter, there's joy everywhere.

Witticisms hidden in every frond,
Nature's jesters, of which we're so fond.
A jolly rustle and a giggle of leaves,
Echoes of humor that the woodland weaves.

## Needles of Humor in the Forest

In a grove where the squirrels play,
Each needle's a punchline that brightens the day.
Like pranks in the shadows, they're clever and spry,
Tickling the fancies of passersby.

A chuckle erupts from a cone on the ground,
As creatures conspire in laughter unbound.
The rhythm of giggles, a chorus so bright,
Turning visitors' frowns into sheer delight.

## A Spruce of Wit Among the Foliage

Within the thicket, a jest takes flight,
A spruce stands tall, full of humor and light.
With branches outstretched like arms in a dance,
It welcomes the visitors, inviting a chance.

The tales it tells in a barky tone,
Of guests who got lost but found their way home.
Among leafy laughter, the trees hold their ground,
In this woodland realm, joy knows no bound.

## The Quirky Conifer Chronicles

In a kingdom of cones where the giggles reside,
A quirky conifer leads this wild tide.
With a wink from the branches and a leafish grin,
It spins yarns of folly that always win.

From tufts of soft moss to the playful bark,
Each twist of a tale ignites a bright spark.
The hidden delight in each rustling sound,
Bringing laughter alive in this forest profound.

# The Jest of the Grove

In the grove where limbs do sway,
Trees whisper jokes, come what may.
A squirrel chuckles, running free,
His acorn stash is quite a spree.

The breeze joins in, a giggling breeze,
Rustling leaves with the greatest of ease.
A tree trunk grins, so wise and old,
Sharing secrets, laughter untold.

Fungi wisecrack, sprouting quotes,
Mushroom cap with a pun that floats.
Nature's jesters, all around,
Bring forth smiles from the ground.

The sun breaks through with a bright delight,
Casting shadows, a playful sight.
In this grove where humor thrives,
Nature proves that joy survives.

## Laughter in the Canopy

High above where branches twine,
Birds tell tales over fruits that shine.
A parrot squawks a clever jest,
As monkeys swing with playful zest.

Leaves tickle each other like pals,
While chipmunks share their tiny galleys.
A raccoon grins, he knows the key,
To raiding snacks under the tree.

Clouds roll by with a chuckle or two,
Sprinkling rain like a playful crew.
With every drop, a giggle flows,
Nature's humor, it ebbs and glows.

In the canopy, where jokes unfold,
Life's a dance, and the stories told.
With laughter high and spirits light,
Every moment feels just right.

## Needles of Nonsense

Sprightly shrubs with needles sharp,
Whisper jests, a playful harp.
In the woods where giggles sprout,
Everybody knows what it's about.

A rabbit hops, with glee he bounces,
Share a pun, it profoundly flounces.
"Why did the mushroom sit alone?"
He laughs aloud, his face well-known.

Squirrels debate what nut's best dressed,
Only to find their humor's blessed.
Beneath the boughs, they have a spree,
Nature's laughter, wild and free.

With every rustle, a jovial sound,
Nonsense flourishes all around.
In this forest, so full of cheer,
Life's a hoot, let's give a cheer!

## Witty Woodlands

In woodlands thick where laughter roams,
Creatures gather, making homes.
A fox tells tales behind the trees,
While owls give hoots of witty tease.

The underbrush is involved in puns,
Ants join in, they're pulling runs.
"Why climb a tree?" they giggle and share,
"Because the ground just doesn't compare!"

With each wag of a tail and flutter of wing,
The forest seems to dance and sing.
Frogs croak lines with gusto and flair,
Turning mud into laughter with flair.

In this grove, free-spirited and vast,
The comedy grows, unsurpassed.
Witty woodlands, a scenic jest,
Nature giggles, manifesting the best.

## Fern Frivolity and Tree Humor

In the forest, spies do wait,
With whispers of a nutty fate.
The leaves all chuckle, branches shake,
A squirrel's dance, a wild mistake.

Moss on logs, a comfy bed,
Where mushrooms joke, by nature bred.
A twig snapped loud, a laugh it earns,
While beetles play at friendly turns.

Raccoons prance with comic grace,
As chipmunks join the silly race.
Each bounce a punchline, loud and clear,
In this green world, all jesters cheer.

So gather round, let laughter bloom,
Amongst the ferns, dispel the gloom.
Beneath this canopy of green,
The wittiest scenes you've ever seen!

## Sprightly Sagas of the Silent Grove

In quiet woods where whispers play,
The critters plot a funny way.
A hedgehog dons a tiny hat,
While fireflies giggle, oh how they chat.

The owls with spectacles do stare,
At dancing shadows, unaware.
The breeze, it tickles tree bark skins,
As ants join in with tiny grins.

A frog sings tales of wild delight,
The moon chuckles, a silver light.
Each ripple shakes a grin or two,
The pond's a stage where laughs ensue.

Here stories weave with each soft gust,
In playful glades, we share our trust.
Every root and branch delights,
In sprightly sagas, nature writes!

## The Giggle Grove Protocol

In the grove where laughter springs,
Each rustle starts a game of flings.
The crickets chirp in silly rhyme,
While squirrels plot, it's punchline time.

A woodpecker gabs, tapping quick,
While bushes shake with a feathered flick.
The sun peeks in with a cheeky grin,
As dandelions sway, all in on the din.

A spunky rabbit hops with glee,
In this woodland, everyone's free.
Each frolic, each pun, a joyful sound,
In this protocol that laughs abound.

So raise a toast to nature's cheer,
Where whimsy grows and fears disappear.
In the giggles shared, we find our role,
A merry life, a vibrant soul!

## Nature's Punchlines: A Needle's Edge

Beneath the trees, the banter flows,
With jests as sharp as thorny prose.
A snail slips on a slick old leaf,
While foxes laugh without a grief.

The blossoms bloom, but oh so sly,
With petals tossed, they wave goodbye.
In every rustle, a punchline waits,
As frogs declare their silly fates.

The wit of woods is evergreen,
With jolly trees, a merry scene.
A branch swings low, a warning shout,
But nature grins, and laughs it out.

So let us dance, let humor reign,
In life's great play, let joy sustain.
Amongst the greens, we nudge and tease,
In nature's laughs, our hearts find ease!

## Jokes from the Woods: A Greenery Gag

Why did the tree take a nap?
It grew tired of the sap!
Leaves chuckled, branches swayed,
Forest jokes in sunlight played.

Squirrels chirped in playful spree,
Telling tales of the big oak's spree.
"I'm stumped!" cried one, lost in thought,
While nuts and laughs were surely caught.

Moss tickled the bark with glee,
As shadows danced, oh so free.
"Weather's great for a laugh today!"
Breezes whistled, causing some sway.

Laughter echoed through the glade,
With every pun, the echoes played.
Roots entangled in jest and joy,
Nature's humor, a playful ploy.

## Thorns and Giggles: A Nature's Jest

In the garden, thorns did pout,
But a rose said, "Let's joke it out!"
"What do you get when thorns collide?"
A prickly situation, let's not hide!

A gardener tripped while trying to prune,
He laughed, "Guess I'm not in tune!"
Petals giggled, not far away,
Their laughter sparked the sunny play.

Bees buzzed loud, sharing a pun,
"Pollination? We're just having fun!"
Dancing flowers added to the cheer,
In nature's jest, there's nothing to fear.

As the sun set, shadows grew long,
The thorns hummed a silly song.
With twinkling stars, they made a pact,
To spread laughter, in whispers intact.

## The Silhouette of Sappy Laughter

Under the moon, tall shadows prance,
Branches tease with a sway and dance.
"What did the log say to the glow?"
"I'm feeling bright from head to toe!"

A gnarled stump, full of cheeky charms,
Pranked a squirrel with its subtle arms.
"Can you believe how I got a split?"
"With a laugh! Now that's legit!"

Fungi giggled under their cap,
Tickling tales of a forest mishap.
"Why do mushrooms always win contests?"
"Because they're so fun-guys, the best of the best!"

In the woods, laughter took flight,
As shadows danced in fading light.
With each pun and every jest,
Nature's humor is at its best!

## **Tails of the Tangled Timber**

Amidst the trunks, a tale was spun,
Of a raccoon who thought he could run.
"Why chase the cat? It never ends!"
Just a whiskered game with no true friends!

Twisting vines had secrets to share,
Telling tales born from the air.
"What did the tree say to the breeze?"
"Stop blowing! I'm trying to tease!"

Owls hooted with wise old grins,
Saying, "You'll never guess who wins!"
Squirrels waved with poetic flair,
Chasing shadows without a care.

In the thicket, laughter prevailed,
With nature's antics, humor sailed.
All creatures great, all creatures small,
In tangled timber, they laughed through all.

## A Needle's Quip

Why did the tree feel so spry?
It had a point, oh my, oh my!
With every jab, it cracked a grin,
Saying, "I'm sharp, let the fun begin!"

In the grove, where laughter flows,
The branches dance as humor grows.
Chirping birds join the cheerful show,
With jokes that tickle, to and fro.

A wise old branch, he chuckled loud,
"Life's a needle, don't it feel proud?"
He pricked a thumb and said with glee,
"A little stab can set you free!"

So here's to laughter, full of cheer,
Among the trees, we have no fear.
With every pun, we find a place,
In nature's embrace, we leave our trace.

## Evergreen Jest

Underneath the needles bright,
Whispers float in the soft moonlight.
"I'm evergreen, the joke's on you,"
Said the chipmunk, with a view that's new.

The branches teased with a playful nod,
"Don't leaf too soon, it's a laughing cod!"
Squirrels giggled, their cheeks all stuffed,
As nuts rolled by, they couldn't get enough.

A shadow crossed, it was the old pine,
"I'm not a tree, I'm a punchline divine!"
With every gust, he'd sway and sway,
Poking fun at clouds, come what may.

Beneath the boughs, the laughter rings,
Jokes take flight on delicate wings.
Let's gather 'round, let's strike a pose,
For humor blooms where the wild wind blows.

## Conifer Humor

Why do branches always have a laugh?
Because they root for a funny staff!
As laughter echoes through the green,
Even the ground feels quite serene.

A cone fell down, it said with flair,
"I'm just a fruit with a point to spare!"
Laughs erupted like seeds in spring,
Joyful clinks in the forest ring.

Come gather 'round, let's make a jest,
With every giggle, the world feels blessed.
Trees whisper tales, both tall and wide,
In this woodland play, we all abide.

A forest dance, with puns in the air,
Leaves rustle softly, they giggle and care.
Let's cherish the laughs, let spirits run,
In nature's humor, we find our fun.

## Fresh Frond Fables

Once in the grove, a leaf laughed loud,
"Look at me dance, I'm better than a crowd!"
Wind tickled gently, spun tales of old,
While every frond had a story to be told.

A little sprout burst forth with glee,
"I'm young and spry, just wait and see!"
With roots entwined, they spun their yarns,
As sunlight warmed their leafy charms.

A wise old oak shared a comical plight,
"A ticklish bark kept me up all night!"
With every joke, both big and small,
Nature's humor makes us stand tall.

So come, dear friends, let's share a laugh,
In every twist of the natural path.
Find joy in tales, let laughter flow,
In the woodland wonders, let your heart grow.

## The Chuckling Conifer

In a forest rich with laughter's sound,
Trees tell tales that swirl around.
With needles sharp, a wit so sly,
They crack jokes as the breezes sigh.

Beneath their shade, the critters grin,
For every branch holds stories thin.
As squirrels dance with cheeky flair,
They share secrets in the air.

When breezes blow, the laughter spins,
A chorus of chuckles from tree-bound wins.
Even the owls nod, amused and bright,
In the conifer's realm, humor takes flight.

So come along, don't be shy,
Join the trees that laugh and lie.
In the woodland's embrace, find delight,
Where every needle sparkles with light.

## Greenery Guffaws

Amidst the boughs where humor flows,
The greenery giggles, and merriment grows.
With a rustle and shake, they spread the cheer,
Each leaf a jester, drawing near.

The bushes chime in with cheeky glee,
Mocking the clouds that float like they're free.
With every breeze, they rustle and play,
Bringing joy to the sunlit day.

Mossy jokers on the ground,
Whispering quips that abound.
Laughter rings through Woodland Glen,
A funny parade, time and again.

So tread lightly, let joy be your guide,
In this green realm where puns coincide.
For in every corner, beneath every tree,
Lies a giggle waiting, just for thee.

## A Sprightly Spruce

There's a spruce that's sprightly, oh what a sight,
With a laugh so hearty, it dances in light.
Its branches sway, creating fun tunes,
While squirrels find snacks under glowing moons.

With needles like fingers, it plays a sweet song,
Telling tales where the quirky belong.
It chuckles at shadows that leap and tease,
Unraveling joy with the greatest of ease.

Every breeze brings a ticklish tone,
Bestowing the woods with a warm chuckle thrown.
The mice join in, with a tap and a clap,
Under the branches, they take a quick nap.

So if you seek laughter, come take a peek,
At the sprightly spruce that's cheeky and sleek.
In its green embrace, let your spirits rise,
Where fun and frolic are the ultimate prize.

## The Leafy Laugh

In a patch of green, where the sunlight plays,
Leaves erupt in laughter on sunny days.
With every flutter, a giggle they weave,
As whispers of joy dance upon the eave.

The branches form jokes that swirl in the air,
The more you listen, the more you'll share.
As the wind carries chuckles both loud and small,
Each leaf wears a grin, inviting us all.

When twilight comes, the laughter dims slow,
Yet nighttime tales of humor still flow.
Stars wink down, amused by the fun,
In the leafy laughter, where all's never done.

So let's gather round, where the good vibes thrive,
In the heart of green beauty, feel so alive.
With every ripple, a smile is spun,
Under the canopy, it's laughter that's won.

## Nature's Gossip

In the woods, a squirrel grins,
Whispers travel through the pins.
"Did you hear what grew last night?"
"Acorns dancing, what a sight!"

Trees chuckle with a rustling sigh,
"Have you seen that owl fly by?"
Branches reach and playfully bounce,
"Last night's rain made quite the flounce!"

Frogs croak jokes on lilypad stages,
Sharing tales through leafy pages.
Nature's humor, wild and free,
Giggling roots and buzzing bee.

## Leafy Laugh Lines

Each blade of grass a jokester's muse,
Tickling toes and cozy shoes.
Dandelions puff with glee,
"Blow us out, make a wish, whee!"

Breezes jest as they swirl around,
With every rustle, laughter's found.
The sun winks down, a golden tease,
"Let's play hide and seek with the leaves!"

Mushrooms giggle under trees wide,
"Watch your step or you'll take a slide!"
Nature's punchlines, sharp and spry,
In every corner, laughs amplify.

## The Sprig of Wit

A twig stood tall, a wise old sage,
Spinning stories on the stage.
"Branches bow to shake your hand,
I'm quite the star in this land!"

An acorn replied with a tiny cheer,
"Let's put on a show, the crowd's all here!"
The roots below chuckled deep,
"Watch out now, it's quite a leap!"

Spring's a comedian dressed in bloom,
Joking with petals, brightening gloom.
Nature's laughter spreads like vine,
In every leaf, humor entwines.

**Treetop Tease**

Up high, the branches sway and dance,
"Join our party, take a chance!"
The leaves gossip in shades of green,
"Did you see who's been here, keen?"

A bird pipes up with a cheeky tune,
"Let's rock this treetop, afternoon!"
Squirrels scamper, full of jest,
"Who can parkour? I'm the best!"

Clouds drift by with a playful smirk,
"Don't fall down, you're on the perk!"
Laughter bubbles, they can't contain,
In the canopy, joy remains.

## Jests Beneath the Canopy's Embrace

In the forest where shadows play,
A squirrel told jokes by the bay.
His punchlines flew like birds in flight,
Leaving all critters giggling in delight.

The owl hooted, a wise old chap,
Said, "Laughter's the best—take a nap!"
With acorns shared, they made a feast,
And the jesting grew, to say the least.

A rabbit tripped over his own two feet,
He said, "I'm just testing my new beat!"
The laughter echoed, a ringing cheer,
While the pine trees shook, lending an ear.

As twilight fell, the jokes grew shy,
But the breeze still whispered, "Give it a try!"
So under the stars, with joy in their souls,
They spun funny tales around the old knolls.

## The Verdant Veil of Humor

Beneath the green, where laughter springs,
The bushes hold secrets, and humor sings.
A chipmunk cracked wise with a twitch of his nose,
While tickled bushes giggled in prose.

The ferns waved gently, their fronds swaying high,
As jokes bounced around like clouds in the sky.
"What did one sprout say to the sprout?"
"Lettuce leaf worries, let's just hang out!"

When clovers convened for a punny debate,
They chuckled at life, never tempting fate.
A beetle chimed in, so spry and so bold,
"I'm here for the punchlines; let the tales unfold!"

With every chuckle, the forest did bloom,
Laughter wrapped round, like a fragrant perfume.
And under the green, where humor resides,
The joy of the earth in each heart abides.

## Underwood Whispers

In the shadows where secrets linger,
A wise old fox danced with a twinkle and a finger.
He said, "Did you hear the saplings' plight?
They swear they're growing, but they're just a sight!"

The ferns shared tales of elders' glee,
"Why did the leaf break up with the tree?"
"It found someone sweeter, a juicy delight!
Now it's under the sun, feeling quite light!"

A rabbit quipped, "I'm late for a date,
With the grass, my true love, it's never too late!"
As the crickets strummed their nightly song,
The forest laughed, where all hearts belong.

Under branches, where whispers dwell,
The jokes were spun like a clever spell.
With each rustle and giggle, the night took flight,
Joy wrapped the underwood in warmth and light.

## Spruce Stories

In a circle of trunks, they gathered 'round,
With laughter as sweet as nature's sound.
A jolly songbird, with feathers so bright,
Said, "Why did the tree grow stubborn at night?"

"Because it couldn't parse its leafy intentions,
It felt confused by all the dimensions!"
The boughs all shook with a hearty cheer,
While the pinecones giggled, shaking with fear.

An eventful evening of witty exchange,
As the branches swayed, feeling quite strange.
A squirrel hopped in with a stack of great tales,
Of nuts he had gathered—times he'd prevailed.

So as shadows stretched, and the stars shined bright,
The forest relished in laughter's delight.
With stories spun on the cool evening breeze,
Nature's own comedy brought hearts to their knees.

## Evergreen Enthusiasm

In the forest green, a joke takes flight,
Laughing trees sway, what a silly sight.
Branches giggle, leaves clap their hands,
Nature's punchlines spread across the lands.

Squirrels jest and dance in delight,
Chasing their tails, all through the night.
A squirrel joked, 'I'm nuts, can't you see?'
The acorns all laughed, 'Oh, how can we be?'

Morning dew glimmers, like tears of joy,
Every twig chuckles, no need for a ploy.
Whispers of laughter in the cool breeze,
In this wooden world, it's a fun house of clés.

So come take a stroll through nature's sweet gig,
Where each step brings humor, so big and so sprig!
Under the canopy of clever fun grows,
Let's jest with the flora, that's how humor flows!

## Whimsy in the Woods

Beneath the tall giants, where secrets play,
The wind tells a story that tickles all day.
Giggling shadows stretch long and wide,
While rabbits and raccoons join in as they slide.

A nutty old owl with glasses so thick,
Says, 'Who cooks for you?' with a chuckle and flick.
He spins tales of yore, as the fireflies blink,
Planting the punchlines before you can think.

Dancing with squirrels, what a merry affair,
With puns in their pockets and seeds in the air.
The forest's alive with sounds of pure glee,
As laughter erupts from every tall tree.

So come join the fun in this sylvan spree,
Where humor grows wild and also is free.
Nature's own comedy, a whimsical blend,
In the heart of the woods, let the laughter extend!

## **Playful Pines**

Under the tall spires, where giggles arise,
The trees twist and turn, wearing silly ties.
With laughter in needles, they whisper and sway,
Telling the forest to bust out and play.

Curly cues in branches, oh what a sight!
Even the ferns join the fun at night.
A deer takes a selfie, grinning so wide,
While others can't help but laugh at his pride.

A chipmunk named Chuckler shares a good pun,
'The woods are alive, let's all have some fun!'
While shadows dance round, chasing the light,
Every rustle and chuckle makes everything bright.

So gather your friends in this fragrant retreat,
Where humor and nature effortlessly meet.
Among the tall needles and laughter so sweet,
The joy of the forest is quite the warm treat!

## Fir-tastic Fun

In a grove where the humor grows thicker than bark,
The trees share their tales till the sky turns to dark.
Evergreen witticisms fly through the air,
As owls crack a smile and do the funny stare.

'What did the tree say to the falling leaf?'
'You're really dropping your standards, my chief!'
Chuckles erupt from high branches above,
Nature's own joke in this forest of love.

With sunbeams like spotlights, every critter performs,
While the pines take a bow, in stylish forms.
The wildflowers giggle, swaying in time,
And the brook hums a tune with a rhythmic rhyme.

So come join the circus of moss-covered glee,
Where laughter's abundant and flowery spree.
Here, jests are as plentiful as sap on the tree,
In this land of mirth, come play and be free!

## The Comedic Canopy: Shade and Shenanigans

Under the branches, a squirrel did prance,
With acorns aplenty, he planned his romance.
A chipmunk nearby chuckled with glee,
Said, "Those nuts won't impress her, just wait and see!"

The sun peeked through, casting shadows so bright,
Where laughter was woven, pure delight.
A raccoon with a mask started a dance,
"Join in my antics or lose your chance!"

The foliage giggled with rustles and sways,
As friendships were forged in whimsical ways.
With each playful whisper, the wildlife aligned,
No serious matters, just fun intertwined!

So here in the woods, under nature's domain,
Life's folly unfolds, like a comical chain.
Though we may wonder, while rain falls and pours,
In the world of the forest, humor restores!

## Treespeak: Jests in the Breeze

A breeze blew through, with jokes in the air,
Where the leaves were smirking, dancing with flair.
"What did one trunk say to the other one?"
"I'm stumped by your shade, let's have some fun!"

The woodpeckers laughed with their rhythmic taps,
Beneath mighty oaks, life felt like naps.
"Why do trees make great friends?" they'd declare,
"Because they always seem to branch out with care!"

A gathering formed, with critters galore,
As jokes took root, making spirits soar.
"What's a tree's favorite drink?" they would jest,
"Root beer, my pals — it's simply the best!"

And so under boughs, the laughter grew strong,
Echoing through forests, an evergreen throng.
In this happy glen, where puns cannot cease,
Nature inspires, bringing joy and peace!

## Cedars and Sarcasm: A Nature's Tale

In a grove of tall cedars, humor was found,
With each joke uttered, the ground shook around.
"What did the forest say to the man?"
"Leaf me alone, you don't understand!"

The creatures gathered, laughter their bond,
With witty retorts, of which they were fond.
"Why did the owl bring a ladder today?"
"To reach the high notes as night turned to day!"

A deer chimed in with a smirk on her face,
"Life's better when you're in this wild place!"
Each creature shared words, a playful exchange,
In the woodlands of whimsy, nothing felt strange.

As twilight approached, the tales grew more bright,
With humor unbound under the moonlight.
In this laughter-strewn sanctuary, so fine,
The spirit of jest danced, glowing divine!

## **Whimsy Between the Branches**

Beneath the renewal of leaves soft and green,
Where squirrels craft jokes, playful and keen.
"Ever heard about the tree that didn't care?"
"It thought it could sit and just grow in midair!"

The squirrels threw parties, inviting all species,
With games like charades and acorn-flavored teasies.
"Why do birds fly south?" one asked in delight,
"It's too far to walk on a chilly dark night!"

The branches swayed gently, nudging each joke,
Their leaves pooled laughter like some merry folk.
"What did the root say to the stump in despair?"
"You just need some soil; it's all about care!"

So come to the grove where the whimsy begins,
Each pun spins a tale, like the spin of the winds.
With giggles and chirps in a boughs' gentle clutch,
The woods brim with joy — it's laughter we touch!

## The Jocular Juniper

In a forest so green, where the light did gleam,
A juniper chuckled, a truly bizarre dream.
With branches that wobbled, and berries that danced,
It made all the critters giggle and pranced.

A squirrel stopped by, with a nut in its paws,
Said, "Tell me a joke!" as it paused with a pause.
The juniper grinned, and with a wink it replied,
"Why did the tree get a ticket? It couldn't hide!"

The raccoons all rolled, tumbling down from the boughs,
They laughed at the quip, shouting, "Take a bow!"
Each whispering leaf, with a tickle and tease,
Joined in the humor, a ticklish breeze.

So in this green realm, where laughter took flight,
The juniper's jesting brought pure delight.
In nature's own stand-up, they found such a blast,
A tale of the woods, forever to last.

## Laughs amongst the Leaves

Underneath the tall oaks, where shadows do play,
The leaves got together, with jokes for the day.
A birch coughed up laughter, a maple was bold,
With stories of summers that never got old.

"Why do trees never play cards?" gave a shout,
"They might fold too soon and be covered with doubt!"
The willows all swayed, echoing the delight,
As sunbeams peeked in, shining sparkles so bright.

A chattering chickadee joined in the fun,
"I've heard all your jokes, now let me run!"
Then burst out with laughter, it couldn't hold still,
"Why did the tree refuse to shake? It had no will!"

The grove filled with giggles, enchanting the air,
With roots in the soil, they danced without care.
So next time you wander through woods thick and alive,
Remember the joy that the leaves can contrive.

## The Sprightly Sapling

A sprightly young sapling, so eager to grow,
Had dreams of adventure, and wished to bestow.
"Will I be a giant?" it pondered with glee,
Or sway to a rhythm of laughter and spree?

One day it spoke up, in the breezy morning,
"What's a tree's favorite drink? Something quite corny!"
The winds roared in laughter, a rustling delight,
As the sapling enjoyed its whimsical flight.

"Why did the oak cross the road?" asked a crow,
"To get to the other side, where the grass does grow!"
The thrushes all chirped, as the sun shone wide,
Bringing mirth to the branches, bringing cheer to the ride.

So this little sapling, with roots oh-so true,
Grew up in a world that was filled with the new.
And though it got tall, with leaves rich and bright,
It remembered the chuckles, its heart full of light.

## A Woody Wink

In a clearing full of blossoms, a tree took a chance,
With a wink and a nod, called for a dance.
"What's an oak's favorite type of music?" it grinned,
"Anything that's 'root'-ed, let the fun begin!"

Around it, the fauna began to unite,
As the beagles kept barking, and critters took flight.
The branches all swayed, in rhythm and rhyme,
Creating a party, in the fresh springtime.

"Why are trees great at solving all the fuss?"
The willow chimed in with its magical bus.
"They can always 'leaf' their worries behind,
And branch out in humor, feeling so kind!"

So next time you wander through forests of green,
Look for the creatures who can giggle and preen.
For beneath every trunk, and among every vine,
Lies laughter that shines, and stories that twine.

## Saga of the Saplings

In a forest where young trees play,
They crack jokes at the end of the day.
With branches that wiggle and sway,
Their laughter echoes, come join the fray.

A beech tree blurted, "I'm feeling trunky!"
While oak barked back, "You're looking spunky!"
The maples giggled, feeling funky,
As sunlight gleamed, ever so clunky.

Each sapling had their own silly lore,
From sneezes of pine to a comedy score.
With roots in the ground, they vowed to explore,
The humor of life, forever wanting more.

So in the woods, where the young ones bloom,
They've crafted a world that chases the gloom.
With a sprinkle of fun, it's never doom,
Just saplings, jokes, and nature's perfume.

**A Needling Jest**

A spruce tree told a tall tale at dawn,
Of a squirrel who thought he could yawn.
But the punchline hit like a thunderous brawn,
And the laughter spread, before it was gone.

A hemlock winked, with a twinkling grin,
"Why did the nut not let others in?"
The answer was a nutty win-win,
With laughter erupting, let the fun begin!

Each sapling gathered, branches entwined,
Prepared for giggles, of every kind.
They spun wild yarns, their humor aligned,
A festival of fun that forever shined.

So in the forest, don't lose the jest,
For in every tree, there's humor expressed.
A world filled with laughter is truly the best,
Join in the fun—be a part of the fest!

## **The Giggle Grove**

In the grove where the trees love to laugh,
A willow whispered, "Did you hear the gaffe?"
"I tried to be tall, but I'm stuck like a calf,"
The maple cackled, beyond the craft.

Underneath branches, the branches would sway,
As the trees played tricks in their quirky way.
With sunlight filtering, they'd frolic and play,
Creating a stage for their humor display.

"Why did the larch feel so out of place?"
"Because he couldn't find his leafy grace!"
The audience chuckled, with comical pace,
A grove full of giggles, a merry embrace.

When evening arrived, and the stars took flight,
They gathered their tales, each one a delight.
In the giggle grove, joy shines so bright,
Around every branch, laughter's true light.

## Hilarity in the High Trees

Up in the treetops, where the world is a riot,
Birds pull pranks as if they're on a diet.
Each rustling leaf signals a new comedic quiet,
A forest of fun that will never be shy it.

A tall pine chuckled, "I can't stand still!"
"Come tickle my branches, give me a thrill!"
With whispers of winds, they carried the chill,
And burst into laughter, at their leader's will.

The sounds of the forest, a nature-made band,
Each tree tells a story, the humor is grand.
With a twist of a branch, or a clap of a hand,
The high trees unite in a whimsical stand.

So if ever you wander, take heed of this place,
Where hilarity thrives and laughter finds space.
In the high trees and low, humor wins the race,
Join in with the boughs, it's a jovial embrace.

## Coniferous Chuckles Under the Stars

In the forest, trees stand tall,
Whispering secrets, the night a ball.
Squirrels gossip about acorn bling,
While owls nod and hoot, what joy they bring.

A moose struts in, thinks he's a star,
With antlers that twinkle, he's not too far.
The raccoons laugh, they've seen it all,
As the night air fills with a delightful call.

Why did the tree stay away from the dance?
It couldn't find a partner, it missed its chance.
But don't be fooled by its sad, green frown,
For under the stars, it won't wear a crown.

So, come take a stroll, enjoy the jest,
In a woodsy world, we're all guests.
Where laughter echoes, and shadows play,
In the coniferous night, we'll dance and sway.

# Forest Fables: Laughs Among the Leaves

Under the canopy, stories untold,
The branches creak, but never feel old.
A bear cracks jokes, with berries to share,
While the deer roll their eyes, pretending they care.

Why did the tree cross the road, you see?
To leaf behind the stress and be free!
The brook giggles, trickling along,
As fables unfold, nature's own song.

The fox tells tales of a trickster's fate,
While the shy raccoon debates on a plate.
Laughter erupts; oh, what a sight,
As friends gather 'round in the soft moonlight.

So take note, dear wanderer, and please don't pout,
In the forest's warmth, joy's what it's about.
Every rustling leaf and critter's grin,
Holds stories of chuckles where fun will begin.

## A Riddle Wrapped in Greenery

In the thick of the woods, a riddle lies,
Why do the trees wear emerald ties?
To spruce up the forest and have a laugh,
With punchlines tucked in each scenic path.

What do you call a bear with no teeth?
A gummy grizzly, oh what a wreath!
While brambles tickle and branches sway,
Nature's jokes float, keeping gloom at bay.

A wise old tree, with bark quite grand,
Told tales of laughter that never did land.
Why did the sapling refuse to grow?
It was too **rooted** in comedy to show!

So wander these woods, see the humor thrive,
Where every creation is clever and alive.
In this green paradise, riddles do twirl,
As giggles and chortles make our minds whirl.

## Aromatic Antics of the Woods

In the shade of the tall, leafy greens,
Laughter rises like pine-scented streams.
Chipmunks dance in the fragrant air,
While the wise, old owl just stops to stare.

Why did the herb call out to the tree?
"Let's thyme together, just you and me!"
Crickets chirp in a rhythmic beat,
Adding to the humor, oh what a feat.

The flowers giggle, wearing their hues,
While the stream's splash joins in with the blues.
Moths flutter by, sporting silly masks,
In this aromatic realm, fun is what lasts.

So join in the frolic, the whispering pines,
For foolishness blooms where sunlight shines.
A forest of antics, fresh scents in play,
Where laughter and joy brighten the day.

## Bark and Banter

In the forest, a dog barks loud,
Chasing squirrels like he's quite proud.
His tail wags fast, his jokes fall flat,
Yet he'll always find a way to chat.

A tree with a laugh, its branches sway,
Whispers secrets in a silly way.
Leaves chuckle softly in gentle breeze,
While critters join in with their teasing pleas.

A raccoon strolls in with a witty grin,
He's got stories, where do we begin?
With a cap full of nuts and a twinkle in eye,
He cracks a joke, passing by with a sigh.

Laughter rings through the cozy wood,
Every creature gives their best, as they should.
In this merry glen where friendships bloom,
The punchlines echo, dispelling all gloom.

## Fir Folly

At the heart of the woods, a fir tree stands,
Telling tall tales with its waving hands.
It jokes about heights and its pointy crown,
While squirrels giggle, tumbling down.

A woodpecker taps with a rhythm that's sweet,
Creating a tune that's hard to beat.
Its jokes are like drumming on the bark,
Echoing laughter, igniting a spark.

A hedgehog waddles in, trying to dance,
With spines that wiggle, it takes a chance.
"I may not be smooth, but I'm full of glee!"
It says with a smile, "Just watch and see!"

As dusk paints the sky in shades of gold,
The laughter grows warm, the night's tales unfold.
In the land of whimsy, where creatures abound,
Every chuckle and snicker can surely astound.

## **Pinecone Patter**

Underneath where the tall trees stand,
Lies a treasure trove in the soft, warm sand.
Pinecones giggle, all in a heap,
Whispering secrets, no one will keep.

A squirrel pops up, stealing the show,
With a comedic flair, it's quite the pro.
"Hey, I've got jokes, but I need a fee,
Just share my snacks and you'll laugh with me!"

Branches above sway with utmost grace,
As leaves play hide-and-seek, they quicken the pace.
An acorn shouts from its cozy bed,
"Why do we roll? It's easier to tread!"

With nature's comedy, we laugh and roam,
In every crack and creak, we find a home.
The night brings a show, full of quirky cheers,
As we celebrate laughter, banishing fears.

## Thicket Thoughtfulness

In the thicket where shadows play tricks,
Branches wiggle, performing their flicks.
A wise old owl, perched high on a limb,
Says, "Stick around, or you might just swim!"

Bushes rustle, a rabbit hops by,
With a cheeky grin and a playful sigh.
"Why hop on one foot when you can do two?
Join in the dance, we've got jokes for you!"

Fungi giggle, hiding under the leaves,
With smiles so wide, they're hard to believe.
"Why did the mushroom go to the party?"
"Because he's a fungi, living all hearty!"

As dusk settles down in the playful wood,
Nature hums softly, feeling quite good.
With every chuckle, the thicket grows bright,
In a world filled with wonder, it's all pure delight.

## **Grins in the Greenery**

In the shade a squirrel plays,
Chasing shadows in a daze.
With acorn hats, they strut and dance,
Nature's stage, a silly chance.

Birds chirp jokes that make trees shake,
Underneath, the ground does quake.
Frolics in the leafy light,
Laughter echoes, oh what a sight!

## Forest Funnies

A rabbit jumps, then trips on roots,
Wearing mismatched, tiny boots.
The fox laughs loud, "You've lost your grace!"
"Just practicing my hopping base!"

Under boughs, the fawns do play,
With sticks and stones, they make their way.
"Why did you cross?" they jest and tease,
"Because the grass was greener, please!"

## The Tree's Teasing Touch

A branch sways down to say hello,
"Come dance beneath the sun's bright glow!"
While mushrooms giggle in the dirt,
Telling jokes, all without a shirt.

The mossy floor is soft and grand,
As critters gather, hand in hand.
"Why is nature such a hoot?"
"Because it throws surprises on a root!"

## A Whiff of Wit

The wind carries a fragrant jest,
Whispers of laughter, feeling blessed.
With scents of pine, and jokes so clear,
Nature's punchlines bring us cheer!

A ladybug plays peek-a-boo,
"Don't squish me, I'm not a shoe!"
Throughout the woods, the giggles soar,
As even tree trunks crack a score!

## Sprout Snickers

In the forest where laughs abound,
Saplings dance without a sound.
They giggle in green, a joyful sight,
Whispering jokes that take flight.

Why did the twig refuse to bend?
It didn't want to break, my friend!
With a chuckle, it stood so tall,
Bouncing laughter off the wall.

A nut fell down, thought it was funny,
Said, "I'm just trying to get some honey!"
But the bees buzzed and flew away,
Leaving the nut to ponder its stay.

Among the branches, humor flows,
Jokes sprout up like fresh green bows.
So when you wander in the trees,
Listen closely, join the tease.

## Verdure Verses

In emerald fields where colors blend,
Laughter rustles, around the bend.
"What's a tree's favorite type of joke?"
"One that leaves them happily woke!"

Leaves sway lightly, tickled by breeze,
Giggling softly, aiming to please.
"I told a branch about my plight,
It just stood there, what a sight!"

Pine cones chuckle from high above,
Spreading joy like a tree-hugging glove.
"Why did the stump sit out the race?
It knew it was just taking space!"

In the chorus of the woods so wide,
Nature's humor can't be denied.
So let's laugh with the greenery's cheer,
And spread good vibes, year after year.

## The Humor of Needles

Underneath the boughs so green,
Snickers sprinkle in between.
"Why do needles never get tired?"
"Because they're always well wired!"

Sharp wit flows like a gentle stream,
Needles chuckle with a gleam.
"Who's the tree's favorite comedian?
A stand-up that's always been leafy-gen!"

In the shade where shadows play,
A wise old trunk begins to say,
"Careful with your jokes, my dear,
One wrong pun could start a smear!"

So join the revelry, don't be shy,
Among the needles, spirits fly.
For laughter grows in every twist,
Just hug a tree and join the list.

## Coniferous Capers

In the land of tall spires,
Laughter shimmers like quick fires.
"Why did the fir always stay calm?
Because its humor was the real balm!"

With branches waving, they share a tale,
Of aspiring trees who set to sail.
"Why don't we ever hear a pine speak?
Because they're busy being unique!"

Needles prickle and poke with glee,
Telling puns just like a bee.
"Did you hear about the tree that flew?
It just wanted a bird's-eye view!"

So frolic here in forest fun,
Join the conifers, everyone!
Where humor grows and roots run deep,
Laughter's harvest, forever we reap.

## Treetop Tickle

In the canopy, giggles grow,
Where critters dance in a merry show.
Squirrels sneak with acorn hats,
Cracking jokes like playful chats.

Branching out in laughter's spree,
Whispers echo through each tree.
Nature's jesters, ever spry,
Share a chuckle as leaves fly.

Swinging limbs, a slapstick quest,
Frogs in bowties think they're the best.
While branches shake with pure delight,
Under stars, they laugh all night.

With a twist and a playful leap,
The forest's secrets leap from sleep.
Giggling leaves, a playful breeze,
Nature's humor puts us at ease.

## **Forest Chuckles**

Amidst the trunks, the laughter swells,
As owls share stories, ringing bells.
Trees stretch tall, their branches grin,
While mushrooms giggle, spin and spin.

Woodpeckers tap a funny beat,
Finding rhythm with flappy feet.
Bears in bowties, clumsy and round,
Trip over roots—such joy is found!

The creek joins in with splashes bright,
Rippling jokes in the soft moonlight.
The breeze brings whispers, a ticklish dance,
Nature's jesters seize their chance.

Sunbeams wink through the leafy maze,
Bringing chuckles in golden rays.
Every shadow wears a grin,
The giggling woods invite you in.

## **Jests of the Green**

In the emerald realm, the laughter stirs,
Bumblebees buzzing like tiny furs.
Joking ladybugs, spots aglow,
Play tag with dandelions in a row.

Twisting vines with punchlines tight,
Wrap around trees in sheer delight.
Raccoons wear masks, sly and spry,
While woodchucks chuckle, oh my, oh my!

Bark-skin trees get the last laugh,
As squirrels unleash their nutty math.
With every stomp, the ground quakes,
As laughter bubbles and softly breaks.

Chirping crickets, a chorus hum,
Join the fun, don't be so glum.
In the green, humor's alive,
A playful dream where all survive.

## **Verdant Vibes**

In the lush expanse, a jest awaits,
Where laughter dances through golden gates.
Twisting vines, with mischief imparts,
Playful whispers warm our hearts.

Nuts on branches, all stacked high,
Squirrels scheme with a cheeky eye.
While flowers bloom, their petals tease,
Winking gently in the spring breeze.

With every leaf, a giggle grows,
Tickling roots where wildness flows.
Mice with jokes on their tiny lips,
Share cheeky tales of failed trips.

In the shadows where creatures gleam,
Life unfurls like a fanciful dream.
Nature's humor, green and bright,
Fills the woods with pure delight.

## **Nature's Trivial Pursuits**

In the forest where squirrels play,
They often confuse the acorns' sway.
"Do we hide them low or high?" they ask,
As they embark on their nutty task.

The rabbits jump in silly lines,
Count the clouds, assign them signs.
"Is that one a pillow, soft and bright?"
They dream of naps in daylight's flight.

The owl hoots jokes from the old oak tree,
"Who cooks for you?"—a punny plea.
Beneath its bark, the laughter grew,
Nature's comedy, just for you.

With each breeze, the leaves partake,
In a dance that's bound to make you shake.
"Why did the tree hide from the sun?"
"Because it thought it wasn't fun!"

## Wooded Wonders

A woodland sprite with shoes too tight,
Danced around till the morning light.
"Why bloom in spring?" it giggled loud,
"When I can be the laughing crowd!"

The log was used for a grand parade,
Where the critters cheered and the sun delayed.
"We'll stump our friends with jokes galore!"
And nature laughed forevermore.

Near the stream where the frogs all croak,
A punchline slips like a slippery joke.
"Why jump so high?" one asked in glee,
"Because the sky's my comedy spree!"

The trees leaned in, eavesdropping close,
On humor brewed like a coffee dose.
"Two branches walk into a bar!" a tease,
The laughter echoed through the leaves with ease.

## Ridge Riddles

Up on the ridge where the tall grass grows,
A riddle spins where the cool wind blows.
"What has roots as deep as the sky?"
The mountains giggle, "We'll tell you why!"

Silly shadows of what's to come,
Tickling rocks like a cheeky drum.
"What's the tallest joke?" the pines inquire,
"Just stand still and reach for higher!"

The peaks wear caps of snowy fluff,
While squirrels debate if they've seen enough.
"Why climb so high?" one chirps with a grin,
"To get the best view of the fun we're in!"

With giggles echoing down the trails,
The ridge tells secrets where laughter sails.
"Let's roll down!" the brave ones shout,
They tumble, they giggle—no room for doubt!

## A Whimsical Grove

In a grove where whimsy takes its flight,
The fireflies twinkle, bringing delight.
"Did you hear the joke about the tree?"
"Of course, it's rooted in history!"

Mushrooms dance with polka dots,
While the breeze tells tales of funny plots.
"Why don't we ever tell secrets here?"
"Because the leaves might just shed a tear!"

A frolicsome bee buzzes by for fun,
"It's not the honey, it's laughter we run!"
With every petal that tickles the ground,
The joy of nature is all around.

So join the squirrels on a merry quest,
In this grove of laughter, where all are blessed.
"Why lay low when you can stand tall?"
In this whimsical world, there's room for all!

## Tangles of Humor

In the forest, laughter grows,
With each twist, the humor flows.
Trees whisper jokes, oh so spry,
Giggling branches, reaching high.

Squirrels plot their next great jest,
Gathering nuts, they think they're best.
With acorns tossed, they take a chance,
A comic dance, a woodland dance.

The sun peeks in with a radiant grin,
As critters chuckle, chaos begins.
A leaf falls down, like a punchy line,
Nature's stand-up, oh so divine.

Each shadow hides a funny sight,
Where shadows blend, doubts take flight.
Beneath the boughs, the giggles rise,
A tapestry of joy, a surprise.

## The Needling Punchline

In a thicket, laughter stings,
Jokes grow wild on feathered wings.
With every rustle, humor spreads,
The woodland's puns dance in our heads.

Branches sway with witty remarks,
Made by creatures hiding in parks.
The critters know just when to tease,
Their quick retorts bring us to knees.

A chipmunk chirps, a squirrel smirks,
Sharing tales that spark the quirks.
In a world of trunks and vines,
Every moment, a punchline shines.

Nature's comedy, fresh as dew,
Life's silliness brings a view.
From needles thin to laughter loud,
In this realm, we're all allowed.

## A Forest of Fables

In woods where stories twist and twine,
Each tree a tale, a playful line.
From roots to leaves, the laughter soars,
Mysteries wrapped in nature's doors.

Fables stroll 'neath canopies wide,
Where mischief hides and puns abide.
A wise old owl hoots with delight,
Spinning yarns that spark the night.

Amid the bramble, jokes abide,
As critters roll and take a ride.
A hedgehog's spines, a playful tease,
With every chuckle, the heart's at ease.

In whispered woods, the laughter reigns,
Where whimsy flows like gentle rains.
Each tale weaves in a fragrant air,
A forest full of fun, a playful affair.

## Branch Banter

Up high where branches meet the sky,
The trees exchange a witty sigh.
With rustling leaves, they trade their quips,
Nature's laughter, like playful flips.

A crow caws out a clever jest,
While woodpeckers drum, they're the best.
Roots intertwine, holding tight,
In this circle, all feels right.

Sunbeams dance on the forest floor,
As shadows play, they beg for more.
Animal antics abound at noon,
With every chuckle, we're in tune.

Through tangled vines, the fun awaits,
Where humor grows in leafy states.
With every breeze, a giggle swells,
Beneath the trees, where laughter dwells.

## The Lighthearted Lodge

In a lodge so bright and merry,
Woodpeckers tap like they're a-nerry.
Squirrels chatter, oh what a scene,
Making jokes like they're a routine.

A bear walks in with a silly grin,
Orders honey 'cause it's a win.
The moose cracks wise, and all just laugh,
Making that lodge a comedy path.

Trees are swaying, dancing around,
With roots that stretch, never a bound.
Branches wave like they're saying hi,
With laughter echoing up to the sky.

So if you need some good old cheer,
Come to the lodge, there's fun here, dear!
Grab your friends, let joy confess,
Laughter's the key to happiness!

## Chuckling Canopy

Underneath the big green shade,
Trees giggle in a leafy parade.
Branches twist, oh what a show,
Telling tales only trees can know.

A raccoon sneezes, what a sound,
Leaves rustle, they bounce around.
The owl hoots in punny delight,
Saying wisdom's got to be light!

In this arcade of nature's art,
Even the critters play their part.
Squirrels toss acorns, aiming for fun,
While birds make jokes about the sun.

So gather 'round, enjoy the view,
Where laughter blooms like morning dew.
A chuckle here, a giggle there,
In the canopy, joy fills the air!

## **Laughing Landscapes**

In mountains high, where eagles soar,
Nature laughs and wishes for more.
Rivers giggle, splashing about,
While frogs croak jokes, no room for doubt.

Hills roll like a jester's tune,
Underneath the cheeky moon.
A fox appears with a sly remark,
Lighting up the evening spark.

Every meadow, a comedy stage,
Where flowers bloom and laugh with age.
Breezes whisper jokes in flight,
Creating giggles through the night.

So roam the earth, and find the jest,
In laughing lands, you'll feel the zest.
Each trail leads to a hearty cheer,
Nature's giggle, always near!

## **Fragrant Fun**

Amidst the forest's fragrant air,
Jokes linger like blooms everywhere.
A patch of thyme tells a clever quip,
While daisies giggle, and tulips flip.

The mint plays tricks, oh what a tease,
Spreading puns like a gentle breeze.
Sunflowers turn, with grins so wide,
Their sunny outlook can't be denied.

With each sweet scent, there's laughter anew,
Petals dance, as if on cue.
Honeybees hum their own song,
In this fragrant world, we all belong.

So stroll through aromas that tickle your nose,
Join the laughter, where joy freely flows.
In every whiff, find fun and glee,
A fragrant adventure that's wild and free!

## **Laughter in the Loam: Jests of the Wild**

In the grove where critters play,
The squirrels crack jokes in a nutty way.
The fox winks sly with a cheeky grin,
While the owl hoots, "Is this where fun begins?"

The flowers giggle as the winds do tease,
While the ants march in line, they say, "Oh please!"
A toad croaks tunes in a ribbit-refrain,
In the soil, we dance, laughter like rain.

Old logs chuckle with each passing breeze,
As twigs tickle toes of the hapless bees.
"Don't leaf too soon!" yell the blades of grass,
"Join us for fun, let good times amass!"

In the nature's party, where giggles abound,
Every rustle and shuffle spreads joy all around.
Get lost in the mirth, let your worries go,
For in this wild jest, we're free to grow.

## Quips of the Quaking Pines

Quaking trees whisper riddles so sly,
"What does a leaf say to the sky?"
The boughs dance lightly, a glorious shimmy,
As they crack up at clouds looking so scrimmy.

A chipmunk chimes in, all puffed with delight,
"Why don't trees ever get lost in the night?"
They laugh and they nod, truth as clear as day,
"Because they always know how to branch out and play!"

The sunbeams nod, shining smiles from above,
While petals perform, twirling with love.
What's green and giggles, can you guess what it is?
A comedy tree, bringing life to the fizz!

Nightfall brings whispers of humor so bright,
Crickets chirp jokes, adding joy to the night.
In this wooded theater, where spirits align,
Nature's own laughter makes us feel divine.

## Nature's Jest: Laughter Under the Boughs

Underneath the branches, we gather and cheer,
For a clumsy raccoon stole a pie from the seer.
The trees shake with laughter, their leaves softly sway,
As the creatures unite for a jubilant play.

A bee buzzes by with a wink in its flight,
"Why did the flower refuse to take flight?"
"Caught up in weeds, that's her excuse,
But she's just a shy one, with little to loose!"

The brook chuckles gently, reflecting the scene,
Where posies wear faces, cheerful and keen.
"Do you hear that grass? It just told a tale!
About how it lost in a race with the snail!"

As moonlight glimmers through a canopy vast,
The jokes keep coming, they're growing steadfast.
In nature's embrace, where funny meets tune,
We find our own laughter, below sun and moon.

## Greenery Gags and Nature Laughs

In the green glade where wild things play,
A hedgehog cracks jokes in the funniest way.
"Why can't you trust trees? They're always a bit shady!"
Each giggle contagious, each pun so wavy.

With ferns as the audience, and petals as fans,
A butterfly flutters, "Why don't we start a band?"
The flowers all blushed, in colors so bright,
As the sun beamed down, spreading warmth and light.

The critters convene, under the sky's vast dome,
Where laughter echoes like a sweet melody home.
In the heart of the forest, joy reigns supreme,
Turning every leaf into a whimsical dream.

So let's toast to the grass, the rocks, and the trees,
For they share a humor as light as the breeze.
A chuckle, a giggle, let's lighten the load,
In this playful kingdom, where laughter's bestowed.

www.ingramcontent.com/pod-product-compliance
Lightning Source LLC
Chambersburg PA
CBHW051700160426
43209CB00004B/965